Pat's Wig

© 1998 Calvert School, Inc.
All rights reserved.

Pat's Wig

Story by
Connie McCallister

Illustrations by
Marjorie Noll

The pretty wig is so big!

Pat is not big. She is little.

The wig will not fit Pat.

Pat is sad.

Tad will come to help.

Can Tad fit the wig?

Tad will pin the pretty wig.
Tad will fit it.

Pat is not sad.

____Macie____

has read this book to

____Mom____